Picture credits:
l: Left, r: Right, t: Top, b: Bottom, c: Centre

Front Cover t Simon Phipps/Istockphoto, Front Cover mt Sebastien Burel/Shutterstock,
Front Cover m Eric Isselée/Istockphoto, Front Cover mb 7382489561/Shutterstock,
Front Cover b Vera Bogaerts/Shutterstock, Back Cover t Serega/Istockphoto,
Back Cover b Liz Leyden/Istockphoto.

Border Images Antonis Papantoniou/Shutterstock, Alexey Samarin/Shutterstock.
Inside Images 6 Alberto Pomares/Istockphoto, 7 t Alon Othnay/Shutterstock,
7 b Hermann Danzmayr/Istockphoto, 8 Elaine Davis/Shutterstock, 9 t Robert Kelsey/Shutterstock,
9 b Chris Pollack/Istockphoto, 10-11 t Joel Grant/Istockphoto, 10 b Luc Sesselle/Shutterstock,
11 b Johan Swanepoel/Shutterstock, 12 Halldor Eiriksson/Shutterstock, 13 t Tim Zurowski/Shutterstock,
13 b Andrew Howe/Istockphoto, 16-17 t Steffen Foerster Photography/Shutterstock,
17 b Steffen Foerster Photography/Shutterstock, 18-19 t FloridaStock/Shutterstock,
18 b René Poelen/Istockphoto, 19 b Stephanie Wise/Istockphoto, 21 t Tony Campbell/Shutterstock,
21 b Glen Gaffney/Shutterstock, 22 Mike Tolstoy/Istockphoto, 23 Marilyn Barbone/Shutterstock,
24 Jan Daly/Shutterstock, 25 Joshua Haviv/Shutterstock, 26 Sandra vom Stein/Istockphoto, 28 t David Danzing,
28 m Lynsey Allan/Shutterstock, 29 t Chris Gjersvik/Shutterstock, 29 b Emanon/Dreamstime,
30 Ximagination/Shutterstock, 33 b Brett Atkins/Shutterstock, 34 Brian Dolim/Shutterstock,
36 J. Norman Reid/Shutterstock, 37 t Q2A Media, 37 b Steffen Foerster Photography/Shutterstock,
38 Biggins Dean/ U.S. Fish and Wildlife Service, 39 t Sebastien Burel/Shutterstock,
39 b Sebastien Burel/Shutterstock, 40 Cathy Keifer/Shutterstock, 41 Cathy Keifer/Istockphoto,
42 t David Scheuber/Shutterstock, 42-43 b Robynrg/Shutterstock, 43 t Silense/Shutterstock.
ALL ILLUSTRATIONS MADE BY Q2A MEDIA.

First Published: 2007

MIGRATING ANIMALS

CONTENTS

WHAT IS MIGRATION?

Migration is the periodic movement of animals from the place where they live to a new place and their subsequent return to the original place.

Birds like these travel in flocks over long distances looking for favourable conditions

What's the need?

The migration of animals usually corresponds to seasonal changes. Most animals migrate for a favourable climate. Birds like Arctic Terns and Siberian Cranes travel thousands of miles for warm weather. Better climate is not just comfortable but also ensures better supply of food and water. No wonder wildebeest and zebras migrate from dry to wet regions for juicy grass. Often, migration is linked to breeding patterns. Many animals, like whales, travel many miles to find a suitable place to reproduce and bring up their young ones.

What About Hibernation and Emigration?

Animals living in cold regions, like marmots, chipmunks and bears, have their own way of beating the cold in the freezing winters — they sleep for months! This is known as hibernation. Animals eat a lot before they hibernate, to put on a lot of fat that will supply energy and nutrition when asleep. Emigration, like migration also involves travel. But when animals emigrate they do not return to their original homes.

Can Migration be Dangerous?

Migratory animals face many dangers, both natural and artificial. Natural dangers include threat from predators. Wildebeest and zebras, for example, are tracked by predators like lions, leopards and cheetahs. It is to safeguard against predators that migratory animals travel in large groups. Storms are the worst natural hazards that migratory birds can face and many birds fall foul of extreme weather each year. Man-made constructions like lighthouses, television towers and tall buildings have also been responsible for the death of migratory birds.

Electric wires pose a threat to many birds who sit on them to rest

Animals like the polar bear hibernate through the long and freezing winter months

TRAVELLING TRICKS

Migratory animals display some amazing characteristics when they travel over long distances. These characteristics have fascinated scientists over the years, and still migration is not fully understood.

Body Clock?

Scientists have often wondered how migratory animals know when to begin their journey. Research has revealed that animals know intuitively that it is time to migrate. Something like a body clock takes clues from the surrounding — like sunlight and change of temperature — and triggers the animal to migrate to other lands. Another amazing feature of migrating animals is the way their breeding time is linked to their migration. Proper timing ensures that their young can travel back to their home with their parents.

Zebras travel with their young ones over long distances, looking for better conditions

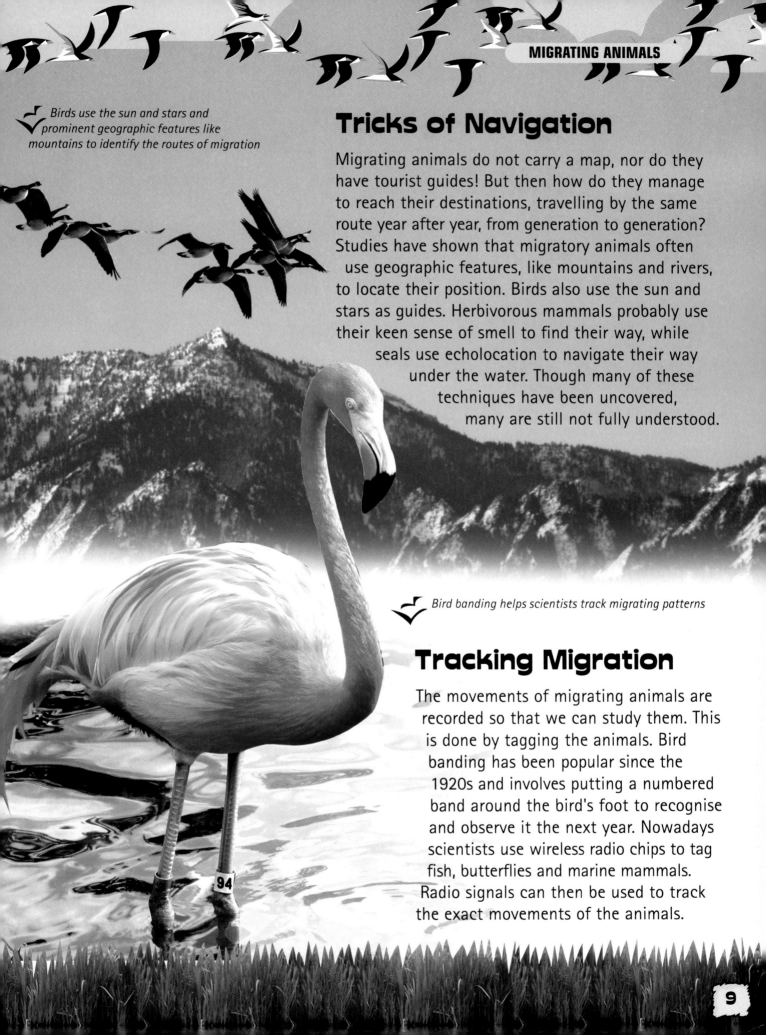

Birds use the sun and stars and prominent geographic features like mountains to identify the routes of migration

Tricks of Navigation

Migrating animals do not carry a map, nor do they have tourist guides! But then how do they manage to reach their destinations, travelling by the same route year after year, from generation to generation? Studies have shown that migratory animals often use geographic features, like mountains and rivers, to locate their position. Birds also use the sun and stars as guides. Herbivorous mammals probably use their keen sense of smell to find their way, while seals use echolocation to navigate their way under the water. Though many of these techniques have been uncovered, many are still not fully understood.

Bird banding helps scientists track migrating patterns

Tracking Migration

The movements of migrating animals are recorded so that we can study them. This is done by tagging the animals. Bird banding has been popular since the 1920s and involves putting a numbered band around the bird's foot to recognise and observe it the next year. Nowadays scientists use wireless radio chips to tag fish, butterflies and marine mammals. Radio signals can then be used to track the exact movements of the animals.

9

MIGRATING BIRDS

Birds form the largest group of migrating animals. Several hundred species of birds undertake long or short seasonal journeys from their homes to a new place every year.

Just Amazing!

Migratory birds have adaptations that help them to travel and survive. Polar birds have thick feathers which help keep them warm. Some sea birds also have waterproof feathers. Birds migrate in flocks. Some birds like the Siberian Crane are known to fly together in peculiar formations for easier navigation. Birds also make clever use of wind currents and use them to soar for a long time without wasting a lot of energy.

Sea birds have waterproof feathers to help them adapt to moist climates

Flying by Night

Though most birds are diurnal, many of them choose dark hours of the night for extended flight. Small birds fly under the cover of the night to escape predators. Night travel is convenient for feeding: Some migrating birds store fat before migration; others eat at regular intervals during the journey. They fly at night, then land to feed and rest during the day, before continuing their journey as night falls again.

Day Journeys

Day migrants include some species of ducks, geese, cranes and soaring birds like hawks and vultures. Soaring birds must travel during the day because they use thermals or updrafts of warm air to fly. These birds usually feed on insects as they travel towards their destinations. Often insects get caught in thermals and become easy food for the soaring birds. Many wading and swimming birds feed at all hours and so may migrate by day or night. Some diving birds that submerge in water when in danger cleverly travel over water by day and over land at night for their safety.

Flying in cooler air at night helps birds maintain their body temperature

Large birds like eagles use air thermals to glide easily through the air

11

WARMING UP IN THE NORTH

Many migratory birds visit the Arctic in summer. In the long days of the Arctic summer breeding birds have more hours to feed their young on abundant food supplies. As the days shorten in autumn and food supplies become scarce, these birds return to warmer regions.

Arctic terns have a grey and white feathered body with a red beak and a black patch on their head

Arctic Tern

The Arctic tern is a small sea bird that makes the longest migration journey of all. It travels between the poles covering about 35,000 km (22,000 miles) in a year! It spends May and June breeding in the Arctic summer. As soon as the young ones are ready to fly, the Arctic tern flies off to the Antarctic. It spends November and December in the Antarctic, where it is summer then. So this bird enjoys two summers in a year!

Small Wonder

Arctic terns lay 1-2 eggs each breeding season. Both the parents care for the eggs and also feed the hatchlings. When they are a month old, the young birds learn to fly and feed themselves. They even dive into the sea to catch fish! When they are about three months old they fly all the way to the warm Antarctic with the help of their parents. The young ones stay in the Antarctic until they are about two years old, after which they migrate back to their birthplace. On the return journey, they fly without the help of their parents!

The Savannah sparrow has a brown streaked body with a white throat and belly

Savannah Sparrow

This little bird is about the same size as your palm but can migrate thousands of miles in a year. They fly several hundred miles at a stretch without rest! During late May or early June, Savannah sparrows visit coastal plains of the Arctic from the Pacific coast of North America. These birds migrate in groups of 10 to 100, generally at night. They breed in the Arctic.

For its nest, the Arctic tern digs a hole in the ground and lines it with grass and other soft material

CREATURE PROFILE

Common name:	Arctic Tern
Scientific name:	*Sterna Paradisaea*
Found in:	Summer: Parts of North America and Eurasia
	Winter: Southern edge of Antarctica
Length:	30-38 cm (12-15 in)
Weight:	900 g (1.98 lbs)
Diet:	Fish, krill, insects
Status:	Threatened, mainly due to habitat destruction

FLYING BEAUTY

The Siberian crane is a large white bird and has a red patch extending from its bill to behind its eye.

Water Lover

Siberian cranes spend their time in and around water in marshy wetlands, where they dig out roots and tubers. They also eat fruit, berries, insects and fish. Females usually lay two eggs and both parents take turns to incubate the eggs for 29 days. The chicks are ready to fly at approximately 70-75 days.

High Flier

Siberian cranes run into the wind to achieve the lift needed for flight. They circle about in thermals (updrafts of warm air) to reach a height between 914-1,524 metres (3,000-5,000 feet). Then they glide forward till they find another thermal and repeat the procedure. These birds eat sand and small stones to gain weight so that they can cut through any wind that might blow against them!

Siberian cranes fly north every summer and breed in northern Siberia and Yakutia in Russia

A Bird or a Plane?

The flock flies in a V-shaped formation. The leader has to navigate and battle its way through the wind, creating a pocket of calmer air behind in which the rest of the flock glides. When a leader is exhausted, another bird takes over. They may cover up to several hundred miles a day. At night sentinel cranes keep watch while the rest sleep.

The Siberian crane is a highly endangered species and is almost nearing extinction

CREATURE PROFILE

Common name:	Siberian Crane
Scientific name:	*Grus Leucogeranus*
Found in:	Summer: Yakutia in Russia and western Siberia Winter: Eastern population: Yangtze River, China; Western population: Esfahan and Fereidoonkenar, Iran; Central population: Keoladeo National Park, India
Height:	About 140 cm (5 ft)
Wingspan:	2.1–2.3 m (6–7 ft)
Prey:	Root, tuber, fruit, berries, insect and fish
Predators:	Humans
Status:	Critically endangered due to hunting and habitat destruction

While flying in V-shaped formation the leader crane (circled in red) calls out to keep the formation together

WARMING UP IN THE SOUTH

Several species of birds cover long distances to celebrate the Antarctic summer. The warm weather is ideal for breeding and nesting. There is also abundant krill, squid and fish to feed on. As winter sets in around April these birds start flying up to warmer regions in the North.

Wandering Albatross

The wandering albatross is the largest species of the albatross family, with a wingspan of 3 m (10 ft)! They arrive in Antarctica in November to breed and lay their eggs in December. Parents incubate the eggs till April. After the eggs hatch the parents go to sea to collect fish and squid to feed the chicks. Albatross chicks take up to 280 days to fledge. The young birds spend their first winter in the cold Antarctic.

The wandering albatross keeps travelling to the sea to bring back food for its young ones

16

Powerful Fliers

Wandering albatrosses travel 10,000 km (6,213 miles) in less than 20 days! They use the wind to carry them forward during their long journey. They repeatedly dive into the still air just above ocean waves and then wheel back upwards, gaining speed from the speeding wind above. While flying over cliffs, albatrosses use the wind that travels upwards after hitting a slope. These techniques help the albatross to fly indefinitely without using much effort. So albatrosses are able to fly for hours and even days without stopping.

The feathers of the wandering albatross change colour with age. The adults have white bodies with black and white wings

Skua

Skuas are large, heavily built birds. The South Polar skua — the world's most southerly bird — breeds in the Antarctic. It has even been spotted at the South Pole! It arrives at the breeding grounds between the period of late October and mid-December. The nest is made in a shallow depression in the ground. It feeds on the eggs and chicks of adélie penguins. The Skuas migrate towards the north between February and March.

Skuas are known to be long distance migrating birds

CREATURE PROFILE

Common name:	Wandering Albatross
Scientific name:	*Diomedea Exulans*
Found in:	Summer: Antarctic region; Winter: southern Australia and islands in the same latitude
Length:	1.35 m (4.4 ft)
Wingspan:	3.1 m (10.2 ft)
Weight:	6–12 kg (13–26 lbs)
Prey:	Fish and squid
Enemies:	Man
Status:	Threatened

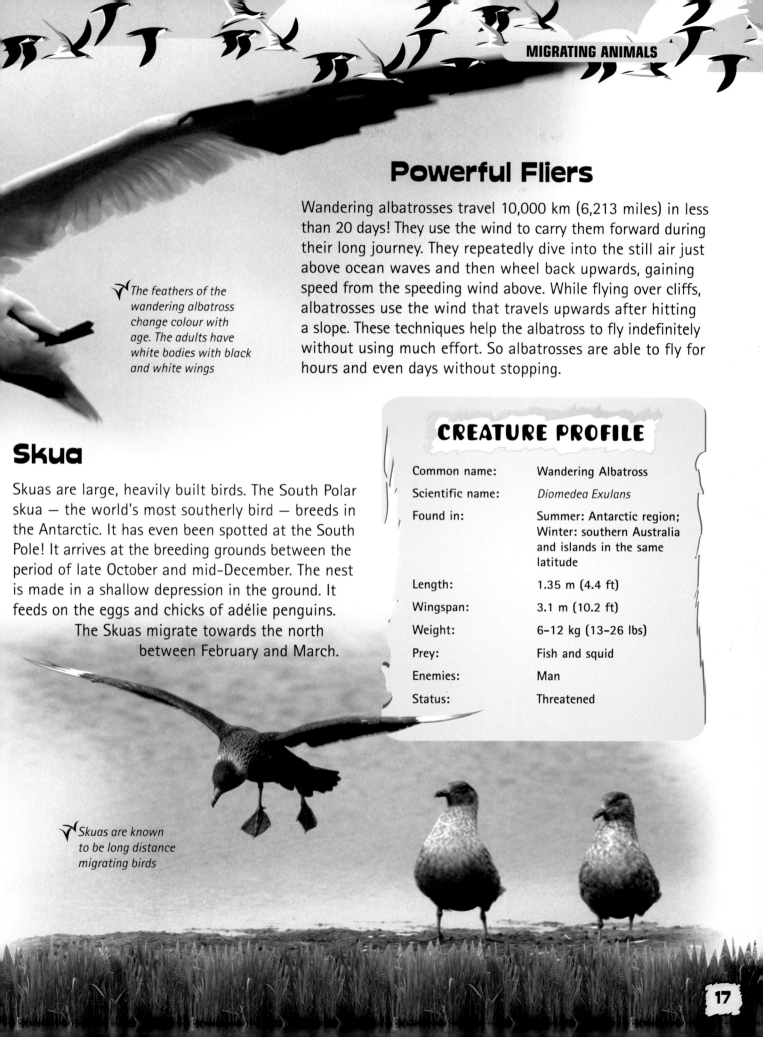

WILD FOWLS AND WADERS

Many ducks, geese and swans move south from their Arctic breeding grounds to escape frozen waters. Waders like storks also migrate from their Arctic breeding grounds to warmer regions.

Snow Goose

Snow geese nest in high Arctic regions from the North Slope of Alaska to the coast of north-western Greenland and western and southern shores of Hudson Bay in Canada. During autumn, large flocks of snow geese can often be seen migrating south. These birds fly both during the day and at night, preferring to fly in clear skies with a good tail wind. If the weather and winds are favourable, snow geese are known to cover several hundred kilometres during a single flight.

Storks have long beaks which help them to feed their young

Stork

Storks are broad-winged birds. In winter, storks of northern Europe migrate south. While some stay in southern Spain, some fly all the way to South Africa, covering 12,000 km (7,400 miles)! If the weather is favourable, migrating storks may fly up to 10 hours a day.

18

Snow geese migrate in large flocks, often stopping together in known habitats

Tundra Swan

The snow-white tundra swan is the largest bird in the Arctic regions of Canada. The chicks are born in May and can fly after about 10 weeks, so that by September they can travel to their winter home in the San Francisco Bay. During migration tundra swans generally fly all night, in family units. They fly at an average height of 609–1,200 m (2,000–4,000 ft), often attaining speeds of 160 km/ph (100 mph).

The diet of the tundra swan consists mainly of aquatic vegetation which they eat while swimming

CREATURE PROFILE

Common name:	Snow Goose
Scientific name:	*Chen Caerulescens*
Found in:	Summer: North Slope of Alaska to the coast of north-western Greenland and western and southern shores of Hudson Bay; Winter: Mid-Atlantic coast, the Louisiana–Texas Gulf coast, and in California and the Southwest in the USA
Height:	74 cm (29 in)
Wingspan:	150 cm (59 in)
Weight:	3 kg (6 lbs)
Feed on:	Marsh and upland vegetation
Status:	Not threatened

MIGRATING RAPTORS

Birds of prey, or raptors, such as eagles and vultures, rely on thermals. This helps them to soar and migrate far away.

Using Thermals

Thermals are updrafts of warm air rising from the ground to the sky. Broad-winged birds can fly in a circular path within these air columns to climb higher. At the top of the thermal, these birds glide in a straight line. They keep losing height until they find another thermal and soar again. Thus the birds carry out their cross-country flights using a minimum of energy.

Golden Eagle

This majestic bird is found throughout the northern hemisphere in mountainous areas. Some species of golden eagles migrate due to lack of food during winter. The large wings and tails and strong flight muscles help them fly long distances at extremely high altitudes. These efficient flyers can use even the smallest and weakest of thermals to their advantage.

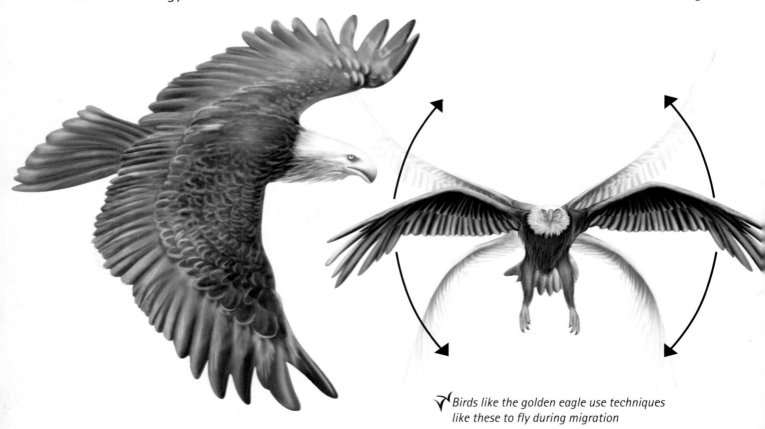

Birds like the golden eagle use techniques like these to fly during migration

20

Turkey Vulture

You can recognise a turkey vulture easily because it holds its wings in the shape of a shallow 'V' when it flies. Each spring, turkey vultures migrate thousands of miles to southern Canada and northern USA. At the beginning of autumn they return to their nesting sites in South America and the Caribbean islands. Turkey vultures migrate in large packs to protect one another. These scavengers can see and smell carrion from a great height, but they eat little or no food during migration.

Turkey vultures rarely flap their wings while flying, instead using the help of thermals to fly higher

CREATURE PROFILE

Common name:	Turkey Vulture
Scientific name:	*Cathartes Aura*
Found in:	Summer: southern Canada, northern USA; Winter: South America and Caribbean islands
Length:	About 76 cm (30 in)
Wingspan:	About 1.8 m (6 ft)
Feed on:	Mostly carrion and sometimes small mammals
Status:	Not threatened

Golden eagles are known for their regal appearance and the power and agility while flying

SMALL MIGRATORY BIRDS

Many other birds, like swallows, humming birds and chaffinches, migrate for food and warmer weather.

Swallow

The swallow is a small bird with a forked tail. When it flies, its tail opens out like a fan acting as a powerful rudder or a brake. British swallows spend April to August in Britain. By September these birds have begun their journey to wintering grounds in Africa — covering a distance of about 6,400 km (4,000 miles). Swallows migrate by the day at low altitudes, at speeds of about 32 km/hr (20 mph) covering about 320 km (200 miles) in a day. They must eat during migration, so they catch flying insects along the way. However, sometimes while crossing large areas like the Sahara desert, they find it hard to find enough food and can die of starvation.

The streamlined body and pointed wings of the swallow allow it to move very rapidly through the air

22

Ruby-Throated Hummingbird

Ruby-throated hummingbirds are not well adapted to very cold temperatures. Moreover, winter means scarcity of food. During this time flowers stop blooming and insects stop flying in their summer homes in Canada and northern USA. So by September, these birds must migrate to the warmer south — to areas between Mexico and northern Panama. Before they return to the north, the hummingbirds feed on lots of nectar and double their weight. This fat reserve sees them through the months of migration.

UNITED STATES
Lake Superior
Chicago
Michigan
Ohio
New York
Mississipi
Texas
Atlantic Ocean
Gulf of Mexico

May
April 16-30
April 1-15
March 16-31
March 1-15

Migration route followed by the ruby-throated hummingbird

The male chaffinch looks beautiful with a bright red belly and a bluish green cap on its head

Chaffinch

This small bird is common through the whole of Europe. Females who live in parts of northern Europe migrate towards the south every winter. This unique behaviour has given the species its scientific name — fringilla coelebs — coelebs means bachelor!

CREATURE PROFILE

Common name:	Ruby-throated Hummingbird
Scientific name:	*Archilochus Colubris*
Found in:	Summer: Eastern half of North America; Winter: Areas between Mexico and northern Panama
Length:	7-9 cm (3-4 in)
Wingspan:	8-11 cm (3-5 in)
Weight:	About 6 g (0.2 ounce)
Feed on:	Nectar and insects
Status:	Not threatened

MIGRATING SEA CREATURES

Many species of whales migrate in groups to warmer waters

Like birds, millions of creatures dwelling in the sea migrate long distances or move up and down the various levels of the sea. They do so in search of food and a better environment, as well as to breed.

Food to Eat

Millions of marine animals migrate seasonally in search of food. Whales, dolphins and sharks migrate in groups or alone following their food, which includes fish, squid and krill. Squid and krill also follow a complex pattern of ocean currents, because the plankton on which they feed occur in large numbers in various parts of the ocean at various times, depending upon the upward movement of nutrition-rich cold waters from the depths of the ocean.

Place to Breed

Breeding and looking after the young is another major reason for migration in marine animals. Female sea turtles swim thousands of kilometres and crawl onto the same beach where they were born, to lay their eggs. Whales move to warmer waters to give birth to their young and then look after the calves in the warmer waters till the next summer. Some freshwater fish swim to salt water to lay their eggs, while some marine fish do just the opposite.

24

Up and Down

There is a major migration going on everyday between the various levels of the ocean. There are many creatures that live in the depths of the ocean, but there is very little food for them there. So every night, they move towards the surface, to feed on the plants and animals that flourish in the upper levels, thanks to the sunlight that reaches there. But these deep-sea creatures cannot stay in the upper levels long as it gets too warm for them there during the day. They also have to dodge many more predators. So they move down into the depths as soon as they feel the arrival of sunlight.

The colourful coral fish travels to the upper levels of water in search of food

FISHY TRAVEL TALE

Millions of fish, both big and small, migrate on a regular basis.
Some migrate annually and some migrate everyday!
Their migration distance varies — some fish migrate
just a few metres while some travel thousands of kilometres.

Travelling to Saltwater

Fish like salmon live in the sea but travel thousands of kilometres to fresh water in order to lay eggs. What is amazing is the fact that salmon return to spawn in the same river they were hatched in! Salmon die soon after they spawn.

Since man-made dams are a hurdle for migrating salmon, fish ladders or channels have been installed in river dams to let the migrating salmon pass through to spawn.

✓ *Before breeding, the salmon changes its colour from bluish-silver to a darker shade*

CREATURE PROFILE

Common name:	King Salmon, Chinook Salmon
Scientific name:	*Oncorhynchus Tshawytscha*
Found in:	Pacific Ocean Spawn in: Mainly Columbia River, Rogue River, Puget Sound near the western coast of North America
Length:	80–90 cm (30–35 in)
Weight:	5–25 kg (10–50 lbs)
Feed on:	Plankton, seaweed, jelly fish, star fish
Status:	Not threatened

26

Travelling to Freshwater

There are different kinds of eels: some live in the sea, others live in fresh water. But all of them have to start their lives in salt water, because female eels only lay eggs in the sea. When freshwater baby eels hatch, instinct directs them to fresh water. It can take them up to a year to reach fresh water – on what is a dangerous journey – where they grow and become adults. Males live in fresh water for up to 12 years, while females live there for up to 16 years: after which they migrate back to the sea once more, where they lay their eggs and die.

The diet of the eel adapts to what is available in the area rather than a specific choice of food

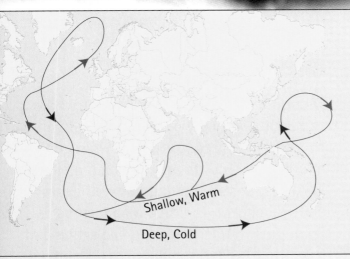

Shallow, Warm

Deep, Cold

The distribution of herring around the world

Sea Migration

Of course, there are many marine fish species that migrate without going near fresh water. The herring is the best example of such kinds of migratory fish. Atlantic herrings are born off the coast of southern Norway, then move north towards their nurseries. Once the fish have grown, they move west in large schools to feed off the coast of Iceland. Then the adult fish return to their breeding grounds.

27

TURTLES AND DOLPHINS

Little is known about the migration of sea turtles as they rarely come out of the sea. Because dolphins do not have fixed migratory patterns it is difficult to study their migration also.

Female sea turtle laying her eggs

Sea Turtle

Male sea turtles spend their lives swimming deep in the sea. Female sea turtles, however, migrate hundreds and sometimes even thousands of miles from their feeding areas in the sea to the nesting beaches. What makes the migration of female sea turtles to the nesting beaches remarkable is the fact that they migrate faithfully to the very beach they were born to lay their eggs, year after year. And they manage it despite the strong ocean currents, their modest eyesight and no visible landmarks. Female turtles lay their eggs in holes they dig on the beach, cover with sand, and then swim back to the sea. The heat of the sand incubates the eggs. Baby turtles hatch in about 60 days and immediately head for the sea.

Orca

Though it is usually called a killer whale, the orca is actually a species of dolphin. This supreme predator of the world's seas migrates behind its prey — much as lions in Africa migrate behind herds of zebras and wildebeest. The orca also returns to its original home following the schools of fish it hunts. Orcas move in groups of 10-12 during this migration.

Bottlenose Dolphin

While many species of dolphins stay in the same area throughout their lives, some, like orca and bottlenose dolphins, migrate long distances. Dolphins migrate in packs or pods of about 12 each. A pod consists of adult males and females, and their calves. Dolphins travel in response to the availability of easy food. Their migration is also dependent on the temperature of the water. Many dolphins of colder seas migrate to warmer waters every winter.

Orcas can be easily distinguished by their black back and white chest and sides with white patches behind its eyes

Bottlenose dolphins travel in groups known as pods and are known to be very friendly creatures

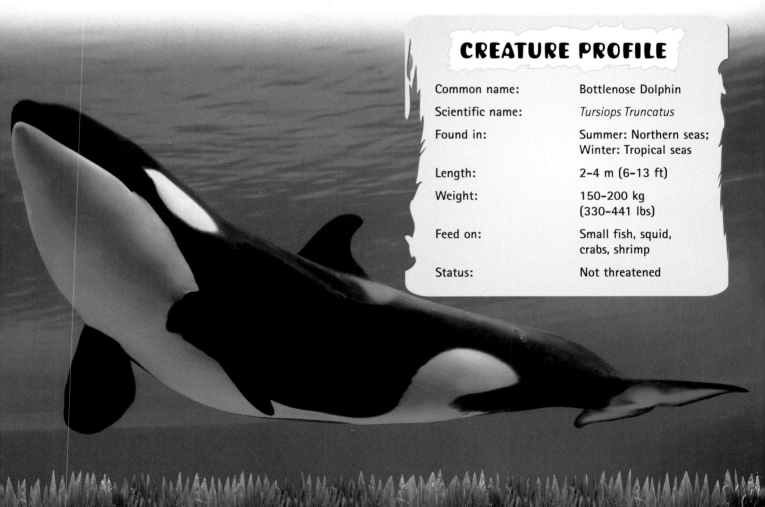

CREATURE PROFILE

Common name:	Bottlenose Dolphin
Scientific name:	*Tursiops Truncatus*
Found in:	Summer: Northern seas; Winter: Tropical seas
Length:	2–4 m (6–13 ft)
Weight:	150–200 kg (330–441 lbs)
Feed on:	Small fish, squid, crabs, shrimp
Status:	Not threatened

29

The great white shark can sense the movement of its prey even without seeing it. This helps it to hunt with ease

MIGRATING SHARKS

Most species of sharks migrate in order to follow food, to find warmer waters and often to have pups. Migration of sharks has not been studied extensively because it can be hard to tag these fascinating creatures.

Food and Warmth

As sharks are cold blooded, they need to swim in warm waters to maintain their body temperature. Sharks also migrate to pursue their prey, who move according to seasonal variations. The great white shark moves to the northernmost part of its range in summer — to the northern Pacific and northern Atlantic oceans — in order to feed on seals.

To Pup

Around June, male sandbar sharks that live in the western Atlantic travel north in large schools, looking for food. Female sandbar sharks, on the other hand, migrate into the bays and estuaries that lie along the eastern coast of the United States, to have their pups. The pups are brought up in these relatively safe waters or nursery areas. The bull shark, which is the main predator of small sandbar sharks, cannot enter the shallow bays and estuaries.

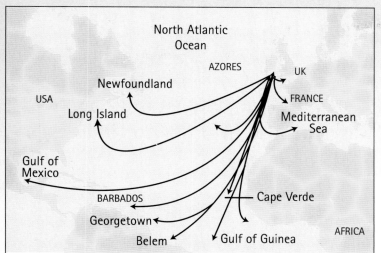

Migration route followed by the Atlantic blue shark

CREATURE PROFILE

Common name:	Blue Shark
Scientific name:	*Prionace Glauca*
Found in:	Open waters around the world
Length:	2–2.5 m (7–8 ft)
Weight:	60–80 kg (130–180 lbs)
Feed on:	Fish, squid
Status:	Endangered due to fishing, which reduces their food supply

The Nomads

Blue sharks are always on the move. They travel about 4,800 km (3,000 miles) each year in large groups. Atlantic blue sharks migrate east across the North Atlantic following the warm waters of the Gulf Stream. They move clockwise from the Caribbean Sea, along the coast of the USA, east to Europe, south to the African coast, and back to the Caribbean.

The sandbar shark moves to warmer waters in the south with the approach of winter

MIGRATING WHALES

Some whales migrate thousands of miles, usually to find warmer waters in which to raise their pups, but also in order to find easier sources of food.

A Long Journey

Grey whales migrate the farthest of all whales, travelling some 16,093-22,531 km (10,000-14,000 miles) in each round trip! Grey whales spend their summer in the cool Arctic waters. As autumn comes, they swim to the warm waters off the Californian coast to breed. Female grey whales are pregnant for 12-13 months and they return to the warm waters to give birth. The parents stay here for two to three months allowing the baby to build a coat of thick blubber, before migrating back to cooler waters.

Beat Them in Size!

The blue whale is the largest living mammal, growing to up to 33 m (110 ft) in length. These giants enjoy wintering in waters of temperate and sub tropical regions and migrate to the polar waters in spring and summer. The water of the melting polar ice packs is full of krill and is the staple diet of blue whales.

Grey whales swim back to Arctic waters after their pups have grown a coat of thick blubber

32

Krill are the main food of the blue whale

CREATURE PROFILE

Common name:	Grey Whale
Scientific name:	*Eschrichtius Robustus*
Found in:	Summer: Arctic waters; Winter: Baja California
Length:	Adult Males: 12–13.8 m (40–45 ft); Adult females: 13.8–15 m (45–50 ft)
Weight:	27,216–36,287 kg (60,000–80,000 lbs)
Prey:	Krill, plankton, molluscs, squid and fish from the sea floor
Predators:	Killer whales
Status:	The species is protected and is at relatively low risk now, although only two main schools still survive

Flip Flap Acrobat

Humpback whales are famous for their large flippers and acrobatic behaviour. You can see these playful creatures breaching, leaping and flipper slapping. They are also known for the 'songs' or sounds they produce under water. Humpback whales spend the summer in Arctic waters and migrate to the warm tropical waters in autumn to breed. The parents do not eat while the mother is nursing. Their thick layer of blubber provides them with nutrition and energy.

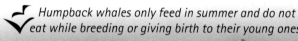

Humpback whales only feed in summer and do not eat while breeding or giving birth to their young ones

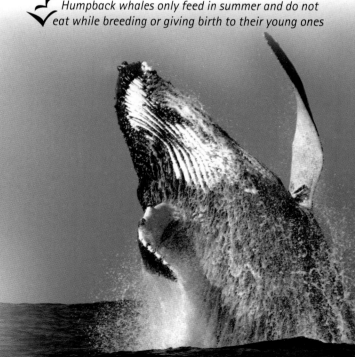

33

MIGRATING SEALS

Northern elephant seals are the only mammals known to migrate not once but twice a year. They get their name from their large size and the loud noises that they make.

Where and When?

Northern elephant seals migrate between the beaches of California and Mexico and their foraging areas in the North Pacific. The first migration happens after the winter breeding season and lasts between 73-124 days, while the second migration after the summer moult is between 126-234 days.

✓ Northern elephant seals spend about a month during summer on the shore when they lose most of their skin and fur

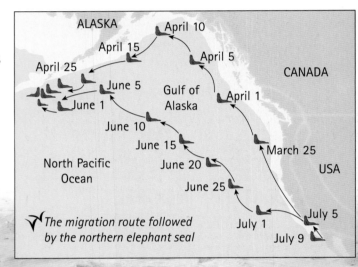

ALASKA
April 10
April 15
April 5
April 25
CANADA
June 5
Gulf of Alaska
April 1
June 1
June 10
North Pacific Ocean
June 15
March 25
June 20
USA
June 25
July 5
July 1
July 9

✓ The migration route followed by the northern elephant seal

34

Life Ashore

Northern elephant seals come ashore and form colonies only for few a months each year to breed, give birth and moult. Pups are born after 4-5 days of the female's arrival at the shore. They are then nursed for about 24-28 days, after which the mother goes to sea to feed herself. The pups stay ashore, at the rookery, for 8-10 weeks teaching themselves to swim before taking off on their first foraging tour in the sea.

Northern elephant seals are known for the long time they can spend underwater when diving

Deep in the Sea

In an average year, the bull or male seal spends an average of 250 days at sea, travelling more than 20,000 km (12,427 miles) in pursuit of food. The females spend about 300 days at sea, covering about 18,000 km (11,185 miles). Northern elephant seals can dive to incredible depths of 300-600 m (1,000-2,000 ft) searching for squid, fish, rays and small sharks! They can stay underwater for 20 minutes. Then they resurface and after a short break dive again. This diving pattern continues throughout the day.

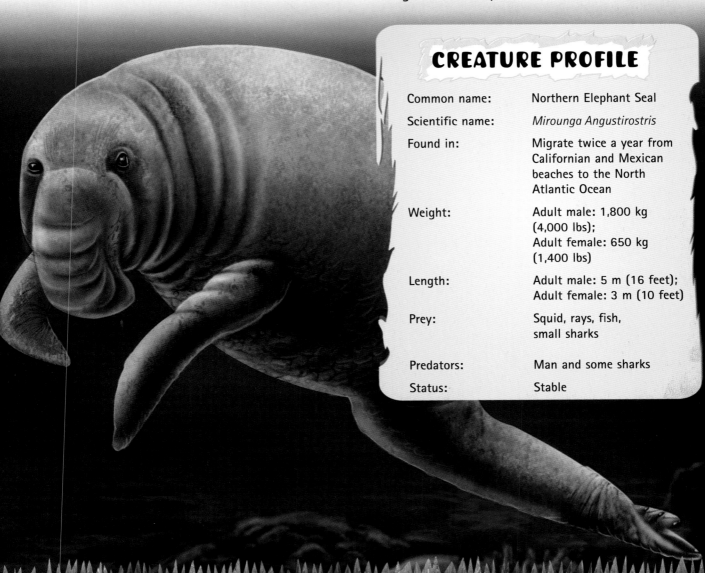

CREATURE PROFILE

Common name:	Northern Elephant Seal
Scientific name:	*Mirounga Angustirostris*
Found in:	Migrate twice a year from Californian and Mexican beaches to the North Atlantic Ocean
Weight:	Adult male: 1,800 kg (4,000 lbs); Adult female: 650 kg (1,400 lbs)
Length:	Adult male: 5 m (16 feet); Adult female: 3 m (10 feet)
Prey:	Squid, rays, fish, small sharks
Predators:	Man and some sharks
Status:	Stable

THE GREAT MIGRATION

In the African savannah you can witness a wildlife spectacle —
a million wildebeest and half a million zebras moving from the
Serengeti plains to Masai Mara, covering over 2,897 km (1,800 miles)!

Rain, Rain Come Again

The migration of wildebeest and zebras depend upon rainfall. Since rains come at different times in the Serengeti plains of Tanzania and Masai Mara in Kenya, these animals move between these places in search of ripe grass and water. The wildebeest and zebras spend December to March grazing in the Serengeti plains. As the dry season begins, these animals move north. They graze on the ripe grass of Masai Mara till about November and then surge back southwards.

Friends Forever

Herds of wildebeest and zebras intermingle as they graze. But they do not fight for food. They feed on different grasses, zebras preferring the taller varieties and wildebeest, the shorter grass that is left behind. Zebras and wildebeest help one another. Zebras can sense predators quickly and start neighing. This also alerts the wildebeest grazing nearby.

Wildebeest and zebras graze together, helping each other in case of an attack by a predator

36

Groups of wildebeest are prone to predators like lions and hyenas

CREATURE PROFILE

Common name:	Blue wildebeest, brindled gnu
Scientific name:	*Connochaetes taurinus*
Found in:	Summer: Masai Mara Winter: Serengeti Plains
Height:	About 1.4 m (4 ft) at the shoulder
Weight:	120–270 kg (265–595 lbs)
Feed on:	Short grass
Predators:	Lions, spotted hyenas, leopards, cheetahs
Status:	Low risk

The stripes of the zebra allow it to camouflage itself in the dry terrain of the Savannahs

Young and Fit

Wildebeest and zebras are constantly on the move, so they have their own special way of giving birth and caring for their young ones. Wildebeest give birth to about 400,000 calves around the same time in the eastern Serengeti plains where there are fewer predators. Calves can run minutes after they are born and in three days they are strong enough to move with the herd! Zebra foals too are able to run soon after they are born. The stripes provide camouflage and make it difficult for predators to pick out foals from the mass of stripes in the herd.

37

FIGHTING THE COLD

Some animals living in extremely cold regions have winter and summer ranges. So these animals migrate from one range to another for favourable weather and food.

Caribous on the Move

Around June, thousands of caribous migrate from their winter home, located south of the Brooks Range in Alaska, to summer homes in the Arctic coastal plains and foothills. The newborn calves also migrate with them. Abundant and nutritious food in the summer range helps them grow fat and healthy before winter. Caribous have large and strong legs with wide hooves that help them travel on snow and marshy tundra. They are also good swimmers, which is useful because they must cross rivers to reach their seasonal homes.

The antlers of the caribou are divided into two separate segments — upper and lower

Big Moose

The moose is the largest member of the deer family. They spend the spring and summer seasons grazing on pond vegetation. This is rich in calcium and good for the male antlers and the mothers. The water helps keep the moose cool and away from insects. As winter approaches and the ponds freeze, moose migrate to nearby forests for food and shelter.

The male moose sheds its antlers during winter and regrows them in spring

CREATURE PROFILE

Common name:	Caribou
Scientific name:	*Rangifer Tarandus*
Found in:	Summer: Arctic coastal plains and foothills; Winter: south of the Brooks Range in Alaska
Weight:	Adult male: 159–182 kg (350–400 lbs); Adult female: 80–120 kg (175–225 lbs)
Height:	1.2 m (4 ft)
Length:	1.8 m (6 ft)
Population:	About 5 million
Diet:	Lichen, sedge, willow
Predators:	Man, wolf, bear
Status:	Declining population, mainly due to habitat loss

King Size

The American bison - about 2 m (6.5 ft) tall and 3 m (10 ft) from nose to tail - is the largest land animal in North America. It migrates between its summer and winter ranges. The northern parts of the range have better foraging, especially grass and sedge growing along the banks of rivers and lakes, which is its favourite food. In the winter, however, it moves south to warmer areas.

American bisons have a heavy and dark brown coat in winter and a lighter coat, both in colour and weight, in summer

39

FLITTING FAR

Monarch butterflies are the only butterflies to migrate as far as 4,023 km (2500 miles)! These insects fly in masses to avoid the cold weather. They are also known as wanderer butterflies.

Female monarch butterflies are recognised by the dark veins on their colourful wings

Bold and Beautiful

Monarchs are large butterflies with a wingspan of 8.6-12.4 cm (3.4-4.7 in). They are also the fastest butterflies in the world. They can fly at 27 km/ph (17 mph) - quite amazing for an insect! Monarch butterflies fly at heights of up to 3,048 m (10,000 ft) and can cover 161 km (100 miles) in a single day! These butterflies are poisonous because the larvae feed on poisonous milkweed. This protects them from predators, who avoid eating them.

Where Are You Off To?

Monarch butterflies cannot survive long cold winters, so they fly south from Canada and northern USA at the beginning of autumn. Monarchs to the west of the Rocky Mountains travel to small groves of trees along the California coast. Those belonging to the eastern populations move to forests high in the mountains of Mexico. They live in these warmer regions up to spring. Ever wondered where monarch butterflies get the energy to fly long distances? They store fat as energy in their abdomen.

40

The stages in the life of the monarch butterfly

Next Generation

Female monarch butterflies lay eggs on the way during their spring migration towards the north. So the butterflies that migrate to California or Mexico the next autumn are actually the next generation of butterflies from those that left the previous spring. But they follow the same routes to reach the same spots. How they do that is a mystery.

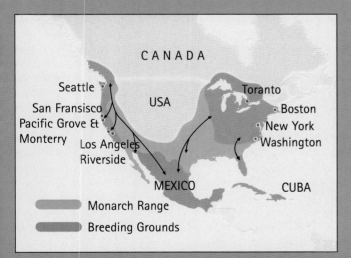

Monarch Range

Breeding Grounds

CREATURE PROFILE

Common name:	Monarch Butterfly
Scientific name:	*Danaus Plexippus*
Found in:	Summer: southern Canada, most parts of USA; Winter: Central America, South America
Wingspan:	8.6–12.4 cm (3–4.5 in)
Feed on:	Nectar from milkweed, lantana, lilac, dogbane, red clover and thistle
Status:	Not threatened

The migration route followed by the monarch butterfly

Deforestation is a major threat to migrating animals and often leads to their death because of loss of habitat

UNDER SERIOUS THREAT

The migratory patterns of animals have been changing in recent years. Migratory animals are faced with threats like habitat destruction and global warming.

Habitat Destruction

Forests are being cut down extensively to meet the demands of an ever growing human population. Humans cut down trees for wood and to create space to live and grow crops. So the space available to animals is dwindling every day. When these animals migrate they find a smaller habitat and a harsher environment. Many are also forced to change their destinations and often die as a result.

Climate Change

Deforestation affects the world in several ways. Fewer trees absorb less carbon dioxide and expel less oxygen. This carbon dioxide becomes trapped in the earth's atmosphere and is known as a greenhouse gas. It is called this because it traps the suns rays and heats up the planet - just like a greenhouse. Fewer forests mean lower rainfall. This in turn affects climate patterns. Since most migrations are triggered by changing seasons, any change in this pattern also forces a change in the migratory behaviour of animals. Global warming is slowly melting the ice at the Arctic and Antarctic regions at an alarming and increasing rate, destroying the habitat of polar animals and also the migratory animals. The melting ice could also cause floods and threaten low-lying human settlements.

The melting ice of the Polar regions is a result of global warming

Hungry Animals

Lack of food is a major threat that migratory animals face. Deforestation disturbs delicate eco-systems and can threaten the natural food chain! As humans encroach upon the habitat of wild animals, domestic livestock competes with the wild animals for food. This forces plant-eating animals to migrate in search of food. This unnatural migration can lead to widespread hunger and often death. Many migratory animals are also threatened due to hunting and illegal poaching, where they are killed for their skins and other parts of their bodies.

Hunting of animals and birds has led to the extinction of several species

43

Glossary

Abundant: Plenty

Altitude: Height

Antlers: Pair of long horns found on the heads of members of the deer family

Attaining: Reaching

Breeding: Giving birth to offspring or young

Camouflage: Hiding from the enemy by blending in with the surroundings

Cold blooded: Animals whose body temperature changes according to the outside temperature

Deforestation: Cutting down of trees

Diurnal: Active during the day

Dwindling: Lessening in number

Echolocation: A system used by some animals to determine distance and direction of objects based on sound

Elevation: Height

Encroach: To move in on another's territory

Estuary: Where the sea meets the mouth of a river

Foal: Offspring of a horse or similar hooved animal

Foraging: To wander in search of food

Global warming: An increase in the earth's temperature causing changes in the climate

Hatchling: A chick that comes out of an egg

Herbivorous: Plant-eating animal

Illegal: Unlawful

Incubate: To sit on eggs so that they develop

Livestock: Animals found on a farm

Mammals: Animals that provide their baby with milk at birth

Moult: To shed skin at certain times of the year

Navigate: To show the way

Plankton: Floating sea organisms

Poaching: Illegal hunting

Predators: Hunters

Prey: Those who are hunted

Pursue: Chase

Raptors: Birds of prey

Rookery: Nesting grounds of certain animals

Scavengers: Animals that feed on dead animals

Sentinels: Guards

Spawn: To lay eggs

Index

45